HERALDRY
The Story of Armorial Bearings

In days of old, even knights who were very bold did not wish to risk being struck down by their own companions in arms. Armor not only protected, but concealed the identity of the wearer. When some unknown decided to place an identifying pattern on his shield, heraldry was born. The author describes how the heraldry became a formal official domain of knights and princes, and later a directory of distinguishing trade marks for families and commerce. A final chapter on "do it yourself" heraldry offers suggestions for clubs and individuals.

Heraldry

The Story of Armorial Bearings

Written and Illustrated By
WALTER BUEHR

G. P. Putnam's Sons   New York

Published Simultaneously in the Dominion of
Canada by Longmans Canada Limited, Toronto

Library of Congress Catalog Card Number: 64-10422
MANUFACTURED IN THE UNITED STATES OF AMERICA
08212

HERALDRY

CONTENTS

ḣ€RₐLDRY

Overleaf: The royal arms of England; the lions of England quartered with the lilies of France.

1.   THE BEGINNING OF HERALDRY

THE TIME was early in the twelfth century, and the place a rolling meadow somewhere in the south of medieval England, which now resounded to the clash of sword against shield, the sharp agonized cries of wounded men-at-arms and the trampling hooves of the great destriers, or war-horses. This was the Battle of Hastings.

Locked in combat with enemy armored knights and pikemen, the outnumbered men-at-arms of Duke William fought to keep from being overwhelmed. Suddenly the Duke found himself,with a handful of his men,

Men-at-arms rally to their liege lord's shield, blazoned with his arms.

cut off and surrounded by the enemy who were quickly closing in to capture him.

The battlefield was a confused scene of swirling hand-to-hand duels, fought in clouds of dust stirred up by the horses' hooves. It was almost impossible to distinguish friend from foe. The closed helmet had not yet been invented; the knights wore chain-mail hauberks or shirts, with hoods that covered their heads except for a small opening for eyes, nose and mouth. Over the hoods they wore close-fitting steel morions or caps, which had steel strips riveted to the fronts and extending downward to cover and protect the nose. The knights' shields were all unmarked and their armor was all alike, so that with their faces almost hidden it was impossible to tell a duke or earl from a squire in the heat of action.

As Duke William's situation grew more desperate his bodyguard began shouting "to William, to William!" in a desperate plea for his men to rally round their liege lord. In the dust and confusion of the battle they could not locate their leader, and a rumor spread among them that he had been killed. Soon panic spread through their ranks and they broke and scattered. Enemy knights overwhelmed the bodyguard defending William and he was taken prisoner.

After he was ransomed, William resolved that never

again would he lose a battle because his men couldn't find him. He had his shield divided into two halves, one half painted bright red and the other white. Now when he wanted his men to rally round, he had only to stand in his stirrups and flourish his red and white shield to be recognized.

This somewhat legendary encounter is nevertheless a true picture of the reason for the beginning of heraldry; it was simply a practical way by which armored knights could be identified in battle.

Although heraldry was first used in feudal Europe and England early in the twelfth century, the idea of using decorated shields, breastplates and standards went back many centuries. The ancient Greeks and the Teutonic tribes painted animals and other devices on their shields, and the Romans' famous Legions carried carved gilded eagles mounted on staffs. These, however, were only for decoration and not used as personal identification as was the heraldry of the feudal knight.

In the famous Bayeux tapestry, a huge pictorial history of medieval life, none of the shields of the Normans and Saxons carried achievements of arms (heraldic designs), and even by 1066 A.D., when William the Conqueror invaded England, he had no coat of arms of his own. The first recorded achievement of

15

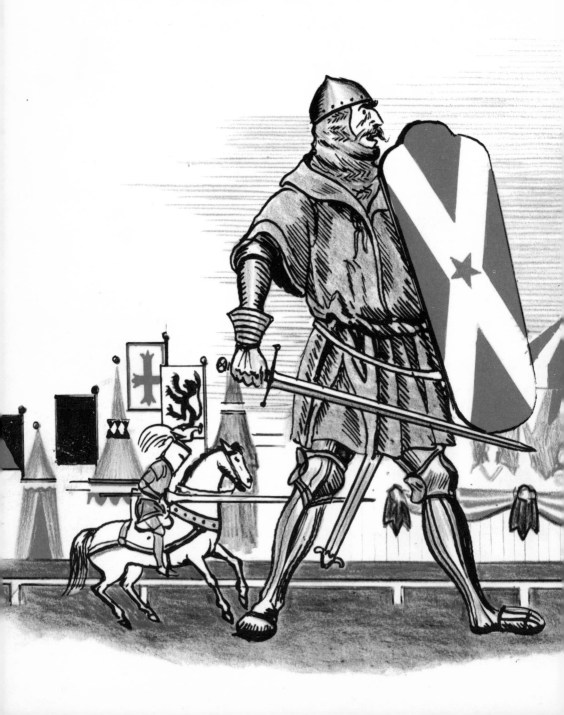

Duplicate arms meet at the tourney.

arms was in 1127 A.D., when Henry I gave his son-in-law, Geoffrey of Anjou, an "achievement of arms" consisting of six golden lions on a field of azure, or blue.

The idea of bearing a shield painted with some simple design which would identify a knight in battle, or during the great tournaments so popular in those feudal days caught on at once. One noble after another had an achievement of arms painted on his shield.

Presently, of course, somebody repeated a design already in use, a situation which would cause much confusion when both nobles were fighting in the same battle. When two knights discovered that their shields bore the same achievement at some tourney, there was as much indignation expressed as if two women found that they were wearing the same hat at a reception. Somebody then had to decide who was entitled to the arms, and that somebody was the College of Heralds, a body of men whose duty it was to pass upon requests for armorial bearings, issue coats of arms to those who were entitled to them and prevent people from showing bearings to which they had no right. Before the Colleges of Heralds were organized a noble could choose his own coat of arms, but after 1400 A.D. he could only get title to bearings by inheriting from his father, or by a special confirmation by the King of Arms.

18

At first the term "heraldry" covered all the duties of a herald, from announcing entries in tournaments, carrying official messages from his master, the king or some great noble, to supervising the achievements or devices on shields. Later, heraldry came to mean the art and system of armorial bearings, and the verbal description of a coat of arms, using the special language devised by the Colleges of Heralds, was called "blazonry." However, to "emblazon" a shield is to paint a coat of arms on it.

As we have seen, in the early days a herald had many duties. He was an official messenger of his liege lord, carrying commands and requests for men-at-arms from the lord's vassals to help in some military operation. He carried invitations to tournaments, or warnings of impending attacks by enemy lords.

When he was sent on an official errand by his royal or noble master, the herald wore a loose coat called a tabard, with his master's arms embroidered on the front, back and sleeves, which was a warning to all that he was on business for his liege lord and was entitled to the same courtesies as his master. Any insult or injury to the herald would be avenged by his lord. In wartime a herald was considered neutral, and could pass back and forth between the enemy armies without fear of attack.

Herald in a tabard embroidered with his master's arms makes an official announcement.

The heralds also supervised ceremonies, such as tournaments, where they had to know and identify the "cognizances" or bearings of all the knights entered, by their shields and coats of arms, and be able to announce the name of each knight entering the lists. At a tournament such an announcement was preceded by a blast of trumpets, always blown by trumpeters, never by the heralds themselves, although many pictures and accounts mistakenly show the heralds themselves trumpeting.

2. THE COLLEGE OF HERALDS

In medieval days there were Colleges of Heralds in England, Scotland, and in France, Germany and other European kingdoms. Today England and Scotland are the strongholds of official heraldry, where coats of arms are registered and jealously protected.

In England the College of Heralds was incorporated during the first year of the reign of King Richard III (1483). The senior heralds were called Kings of Heralds or Kings of Arms. There are three Kings of Arms: one is the Garter King of Arms, the principal herald, who is concerned with the affairs of the Knights of the Garter; another is the Clarenceaux King of Arms, with jurisdiction over southern England; and finally, the

23

The Earl Marshal, head of the College of Heralds, and a herald (at left).

Norroy and Ulster King of Arms, with jurisdiction over northern England below the Scottish border and over Ulster in Ireland. Scotland has always had a separate College of Heralds with somewhat different rules from England's.

Below the Kings of Arms in rank are six heralds: Windsor, Richmond, Somerset, York, Lancaster and Chester. Below them are four junior heralds or "pursuivants," with the picturesque titles of Rouge Dragon, Rouge Croix, Bluemantle and Portcullis. The Kings of Arms had specially designed crowns and other regalia, which were worn only during the coronation of a monarch, during which they had many ceremonial duties.

In England today, the Duke of Norfolk, as Earl Marshal, has authority over armory, and under him the Kings of Arms grant coats of arms to deserving private individuals who petition for them, as well as to towns, counties, organizations and businesses, such as banks, steamship or air lines and many others.

From a simple device painted on a shield, called a "shield of arms," which was the beginning of heraldry, armorial bearings began to be displayed on banners, square flags borne on the tips of lances or spears. Planted in front of the tent of a noble or knight in a war camp or at a great tournament, the banner served the same purpose as the modern name plate over a doorbell does today. Arms were also embroidered on the fronts, backs and sleeves of the surcoats which knights wore over their armor, so that they could be recognized when they were not carrying their shields. Even the war-horses were decked out in brilliantly colored trappings edged with fringe and tassels, bearing the arms of the horse's rider.

A "coat of arms" was so called because it was painted or embroidered on the surcoat. When the arms appeared on the shield they were known as a "shield of arms." Nobles and knights were usually property owners, and so they often had to sign legal papers, but since few of them could read and write, a written signature.was usually impossible. They stamped their personal seals on documents instead of signing them. The seals usually included part or all of the noble's coat of arms, so that anyone could recognize the bearings without being able to read.

A heraldic coat of arms, whether displayed on a shield, a banner or a surcoat, could only be carried by its owner, never by his men-at-arms or servants. The owner could also use the arms on his buttons, brushes, silver, curtains and his furniture. Today livery colors can also be shown by the owner on his house, car and writing paper, and as his racing colors.

Many feudal nobles and knights also had separate

devices, called badges, often made up of some part of their coat of arms, which the retainers might wear and which could appear on their servants' liveries. Often a badge consisted of a chief's crest, encircled by a strap and buckle, with his motto in a ribbon.

Arms painted on shields had to be easy to see and easy to recognize. Colors had to contrast with each other. In heraldry, gold, silver and five colors — red, blue, green, purple and black — were used, and a color was never placed next to another color, or gold next to silver. The rule was to place a metal (gold or silver) next to a tincture (color) or vice versa, because they would contrast well and be easily seen.

By the fifteenth century, when full plate armor became usual, the shield was seldom worn except at tournaments and so arms used purely as identification became less important. Then designs became much more elaborate, until some coats of arms were so subdivided by "quarterings" (of which more later) that it would have been impossible to recognize them in the heat of battle.

Badge

Crest

Badge

Torse

Chapeau

Mantling

Coronet

Helm

Supporter

Supporter

Shield

Motto

Compartment

COAT OF ARMS

3.   THE COAT OF ARMS

Arms still centered around the shield, but presently other decorations were added as a part of the "achievement." On complete achievements a coronet rests on the top of the shield, surmounted by a helm from which hangs, in decorative folds, a cloth called a lambrequin or mantling, in heraldic colors, with a contrasting lining. The mantling of a sovereign is always of gold, lined with ermine. The mantling was originally a cloth worn by the armored knight under his helm and hanging down over neck and shoulders as a protection against the sun.

Resting on top of the helm is a wreath of twisted silk, every other twist of some tincture to contrast with the intervening twists of a metal. This is the torse, or crest-wreath, and upon it stands the crest, or personal device of the owner, which may be a lion, a stag, a flower, or some other emblem. The crest and the shield may each be used separately as insignia by their owner. The crest, in the early days of knighthood, was actually worn atop the knight's helm when he went into battle or when he entered the lists in a joust at some tournament, but crests became so elaborate and unwieldy that they were gradually abandoned.

Peers and some knights are entitled to "supporters," which are two upright figures, one on either side of the shield, supporting it and standing on a mound under the shield, called a "compartment." Supporters may be lions, dragons, unicorns, or any other figures fancied by the owner.

Below or upon the compartment, in a scroll, is the motto of the armiger (holder of arms), usually in Latin. If he is also entitled to badges, these are often displayed to the right and left of the crest.

To anyone who understands something of heraldry, the symbols placed above the shield tell a good deal about the owner's position and rank, just as the arms within the shield tell of his family background. For instance, the type of helm displayed shows the owner's position in nobility.

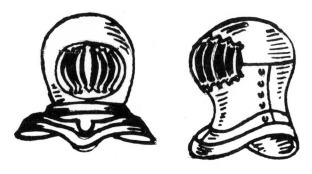

King   Peers

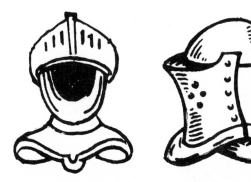

Baronets and Knights   Esquires and Gentlemen

For the king and the royal princes a gold-barred helm set full-face with a closed visor is used. For peers (dukes, marquesses, earls, viscounts and barons) a barred helm of silver decorated with gold is set side-wise above the shield. For baronets and knights a steel

31

helm with raised visor, usually full-face, and for esquires and gentlemen a steel helm with closed visor are shown. In the early days of heraldry there were no rules for displaying helms; not until the seventeenth century were these regulations adopted.

We have seen that a barred helm of silver decorated with gold, set sidewise, indicates a peer. To find out his rank, one has to look to the coronet above the helm. The king's royal crown has a gold rim set with jewels on which are alternate crosses and fleur-de-lis. Above the rim, crossed arches set with pearls are surmounted,

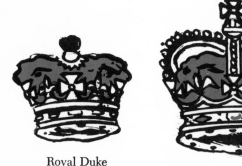

Royal Duke

Royal Crown

Duke

Marquess

Earl

Viscount

Baron

where they cross, with a golden orb topped by a cross.

The coronet of a royal duke is like that of the king, but without the arches, and with the rim carved to represent jewels, but without the stones. A duke's coronet has a silver-gilt rim, like the royal duke's, topped with eight strawberry leaves. The marquess's coronet has four strawberry leaves, alternating with four silver balls, while that of the earl has eight points each topped with a silver ball. The coronet of a viscount has sixteen close-set silver balls above its rim, and that of a baron has a plain silver-gilt rim with six large silver balls. In England baronets bear on their shields a silver shield on which is charged a red hand.

The shields on which the personal arms of their owners are displayed vary slightly in shape. Some are more blunt at the tip. Arms are occasionally displayed on a cartouche or oval, a shape preferred especially by the clergy, who as men of peace prefer not to use the military shield. The arms of a lady of title are always displayed in a lozenge (a diamond shape), never on a shield, except in the case of a reigning queen.

4. THE TINCTURES

The colors used in armorial bearings were limited to five, in addition to which gold (also represented as yellow) and silver (represented as white), known as the "metals," were used. Besides these, the heraldic designers used patterns representing furs, such as the arctic stoat, which in winter turns white and is called ermine, and the gray squirrel. Each fur is indicated by a regular pattern of differently shaped spots covering the field. The tinctures, metals and furs of heraldry, together with their heraldic names, are shown on a diagram.

In blazoning (or describing) a coat of arms, the colors of the various objects on the arms are always described by their heraldic names, but when an object is depicted in its natural color it is always described as "proper." A black raven would be blazoned "a raven proper," instead of "a raven sable." Another rule of blazonry is never to mention a tincture of metal twice in the same blazon. If it occurs again in the same description, the blazoner counts back to where the color was mentioned in relation to other colors. If, for instance, the color of the object is black, and black was

FURS

Ermine   Ermines

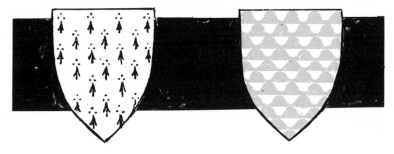

Erminois   Pean

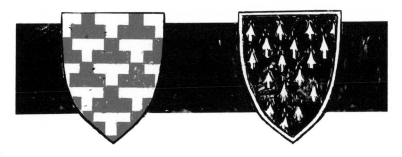

Vaire   Potent

TINCTURES

Blue
Azure

Red
Gules

Green
Vert

Purple
Purpure

Black
Sable

METALS

(Gold or Yellow) — Or or Gold   (Silver or White) — Argent

the first color described, he would say, "an object of the first," instead of "an object sable." If two other colors were mentioned before black, he would describe it as "an object of the third." When tinctures are reversed, they are spoken of as "countercharged." For example, a shield divided in two horizontally, one half colored silver and the other red, with a bend across it which is colored red where it crosses the silver half and silver where it crosses the red half, is described, "per pale argent and gules, a bend countercharged."

POINTS ON THE FIELD

A — Dexter Side
B — Sinister
C — Chief
D — Base
E — Dexter Chief
F — Sinister Chief
G — Middle Chief
H — Dexter Base

J — Sinister Base
K — Middle Base
L — Honor Point
M — Fess Point
N — Navel Point
O — Flank Dexter
P — Flank Sinister

5. THE SHIELD OF ARMS

The surface of a shield is called "the field," and the emblems placed on it are called "charges." In order to blazon or describe a coat of arms with words alone, some way of locating the emblems exactly in their proper positions on the shield was needed. One could hardly say the shield contained a lion rampant "about halfway down the right side."

For this reason the shield was divided into exact areas, each one with its own name. To begin with, in heraldry the side of the shield to the right of the *wearer* is considered the right side, although it is the left side when *you* face it. The heraldic right side is always called the dexter side, while the left is the sinister. The various points on the field are shown on the sketch of the shield, with their heraldic names.

In describing the arms on a shield, for instance, if you wanted to blazon arms which contained a lion rampant in the upper left-hand corner, *facing you* (E), you would say, "in dexter chief, a lion rampant."

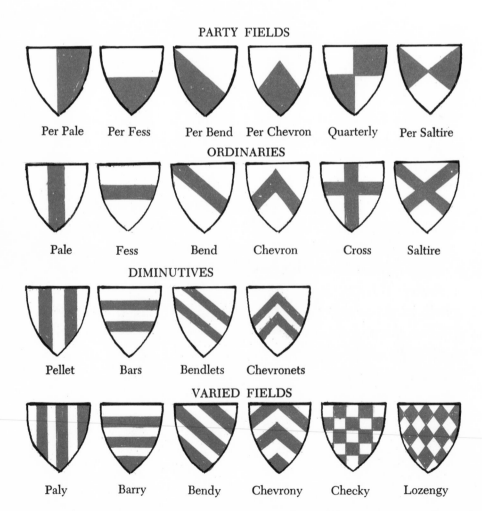

PARTY FIELDS

Per Pale   Per Fess   Per Bend   Per Chevron   Quarterly   Per Saltire

ORDINARIES

Pale   Fess   Bend   Chevron   Cross   Saltire

DIMINUTIVES

Pellet   Bars   Bendlets   Chevronets

VARIED FIELDS

Paly   Barry   Bendy   Chevrony   Checky   Lozengy

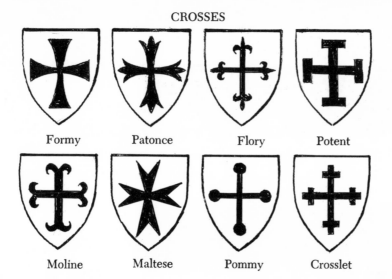

Formy	Patonce	Flory	Potent

Moline	Maltese	Pommy	Crosslet

6. HONORABLE ORDINARIES

The simplest of all shield designs was made by dividing a shield in half, either horizontally or vertically, and painting the two halves in contrasting colors. Later this was varied by painting bars, crosses or chevrons on the shields. Such geometrically designed shields were called "honorable ordinaries." All coats of arms were either made up of ordinaries or of "charges," emblems placed on the field, consisting of anything a man could think of, from animals, birds and flowers, to castles, weapons, ships or windmills — whatever happened to please him. Sometimes a charge might suggest his family name, something in his history or his military exploits.

41

Dancetty

Indented

Engrailed

Invected

Wavy

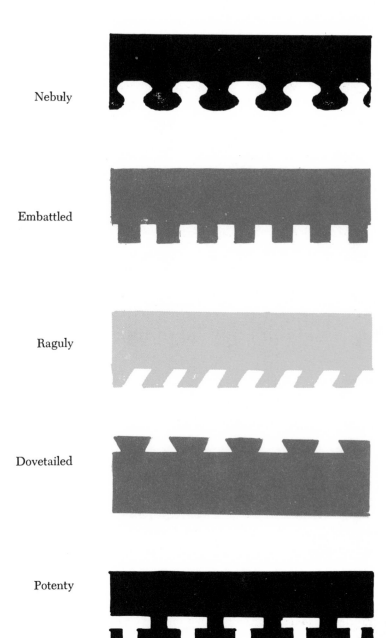

Nebuly

Embattled

Raguly

Dovetailed

Potenty

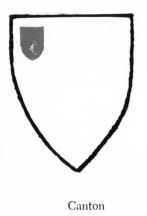

Canton

Pile

Tincture Reversed

Among the ordinaries there are six main divisions of the field; these are the party fields. There are also six different basic "ordinaries," six varied fields, and four diminutives. These are all shown in a diagram, with their heraldic descriptions. Besides these there are many variations, too numerous to illustrate here. Notice that a vertical stripe is called a "pale"; a horizontal one, a "fess"; a diagonal from dexter chief to sinister base, a "bend"; and a diagonal stripe from the opposite direction, a "bend sinister."

There are also the cross, the saltire (a cross shaped like an X) and the chevron. The cross was much used in heraldry because it stood for Christianity and medieval people were deeply religious. Shown are some heraldic crosses, called Formy, Patonce, Flory, Potent, Moline, Maltese, Pommy and Crosslet.

You will notice in the diagram of party fields that when a shield is divided by a horizontal line across the center the field is "party per fess" or "fess-wise"; when cut by a vertical center line it is "party per pale" or "pale-wise."

When the heralds ran out of ordinaries they found that they could produce many more original arms by making the edges of the ordinaries wavy, scalloped or jagged in different ways. In the same diagram you will see ten variations of these edges,with their heraldic names. Below them are two additional shapes often used. One is a "canton," a small, usually rectangular shape often placed in dexter chief, the other a "pile," a wedge shape which may appear in different positions in the field, or combined with other piles.

Another way of achieving a variation in arms is to scatter the field with small objects like crosslets or fleur-de-lis in a pattern. This is described in heraldry as "semé" or "semy."

7. THE CHARGES

Now that we have examined the ordinaries, or geometric shapes, let's take a look at the other half of the armorial bearings, the charges. They are fascinating, because medieval knights had lively imaginations and they painted some strange and wonderful objects upon their shields. They began to take the place of the unexciting crosses and stripes of the ordinaries.

Animals in various positions were very popular. Among the beasts emblazoned on the shields were horses, elephants, apes, hedgehogs, weasels, rabbits, lions, bears, hounds, even hippopotamuses and zebras, which heraldic artists could never have seen for themselves, but had heard described by travelers and trad-

Stag

Lion

Ram

Horse

Boars' Heads & Bee

Gorged Leopard

Giraffe

Elephant

Wolf

ANIMALS IN HERALDRY

Pelican   Hawk   Heron

Fish   Crab

Ostrich

BIRDS, FISH AND CRUSTACEANS IN HERALDRY

MONSTERS IN HERALDRY

Dragon   Wyvern   Cockatrice   Griffin

ers to the East. They also depicted the heads of bulls, wolves, boars and stags.

Among the birds they adopted were falcons, herons, ravens, eagles, parrots, ostriches, swans, ducks and geese. One curious bird, which they called the martlet, was always shown without feet, because medieval folk believed that the martlet, or swallow, had no feet, and so must remain perpetually in the air.

Many shields bore dolphins, salmon, crabs, lobsters and scallop shells; even snakes and insects appeared as charges on some. The heraldic designers really let their imaginations run riot when they depicted the legendary creatures called "monsters," which included dragons, griffins, cockatrices and wyverns. They appeared in all their ferocity as charges or supporters on many a shield.

The positions of these animals and birds on a shield were carefully prescribed, and each position had its heraldic description used in blazoning the coat of arms. The lion was the most popular beast in heraldry and so was depicted in many positions, but he was probably first drawn by some heraldic artist who had never seen a lion and so the heraldic lion was not very realistic. However, he *was* made to look both fierce and brave, and that was what mattered.

A lion standing erect on one hind paw with the other

Rampant

Passant

Passant Regardant

Sejant

HERALDIC POSITIONS OF THE LION AND THE DEER

Couchant

Passant Gardant

Springing

At Gaze

Gorged

Rose

Sheaf of Grain

Apples

FLOWERS, GRAINS AND FRUITS IN HERALDRY

paws raised is "rampant" in heraldry. Walking, with one forepaw raised, he is "passant." In the same position, but looking toward you, he is "passant gardant." Looking over his shoulder, he is "passant regardant." Squatting on his haunches, he is "sejant"; sitting down with head erect, he is "couchant"; and lying down with head between his paws, he is "dormant."

Two lions facing each other are called "combattant" and a halved lion was known as a "demi-lion." Lions colored gold or yellow were described as "proper" but their tongues and claws were often painted red, described in blazonry as "langued gules."

COMMON CHARGES IN HERALDRY

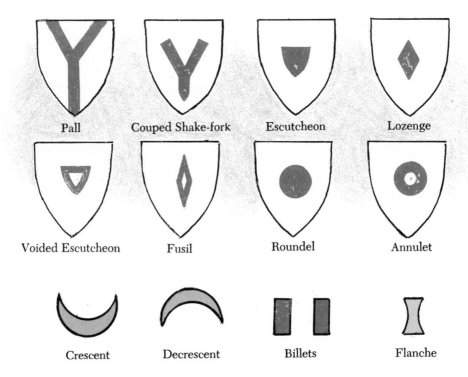

Pall	Couped Shake-fork	Escutcheon	Lozenge
Voided Escutcheon	Fusil	Roundel	Annulet
Crescent	Decrescent	Billets	Flanche

De la Hose   Oakes   Arundel   Bowes

CANTING ARMS

The positions of horned beasts, such as deer or cattle, had different names than the same positions of beasts of prey. A stag standing was described as "statant"; walking, he was "trippant"; running, he was "at speed." A stag lying down with forelegs under his chest was "lodged"; with forelegs off the ground, he was "springing"; standing, with head facing you, he was "at gaze" and with head down, feeding, he was "pascuant."

A stag with horns was described as "attired of antlers" and the branches of the antlers were called "tynes." When an object was shown cut off cleanly, as for example the head and neck of an animal, it was "couped"; when shown torn off raggedly, as, for instance, a broken-off limb of a tree, it was "erazed." Animals shown on a coat of arms were often collared, sometimes with a chain from the collar looping over the back. Sometimes they wore crowns and sometimes the crown was around the neck, which was called "gorged."

Trees, flowers, fruits and grains all were much used by the heraldic designers. The oak was the most popular, and is always meant when no other type of tree is specifically mentioned. Trees are shown both as growing from a "mount" of soil or grass, or with their roots exposed, as if they had just been torn from the ground. They are shown garnished with their fruits when the blazon says they are "fructed."

Branches cut or torn from the tree were often used, and are described as "couped" or "slipped." Ears of wheat, barley, oats and rye are often shown, and sometimes the entire bound sheaf is used.

Early in the history of heraldry, nobles with names which could be illustrated in picture form often selected charges which would suggest their names. These coats of arms were called "canting arms." A peer named Oakley might show an oak tree on his shield, or one named Arundel would show several swallows on his shield. (The French word for swallow, *hirondelle*, sounds very much like Arundel.) A feudal family named De la Hose bore a coat of arms showing three stockinged legs on their shield.

Canting arms were popular in feudal days when few people could read; such a punning achievement of arms would at once identify the owner of the shield, and his name would be remembered.

8. DIFFERENCING OF ARMS

When an armiger (anyone who bore arms) married and had children, his sons naturally wanted to bear their father's arms on their shields, but he was the only one with a right to bear them as long as he lived. Therefore, in the early days of heraldry, each son made some change in his father's bearings, perhaps by adding some new symbol to the field, changing the tinctures or adding a border. This was called "differencing." Thus while each son displayed his father's arms, each son's shield was different and original.

Usually the eldest son, who would inherit his father's title and arms when he died, added a narrow bar with

EARLY DIFFERENCING

Father's Arms

Eldest Son's   Younger Sons'

MODERN DIFFERENCING

Father's Arms

Eldest Son's   2nd Son's   3rd Son's

4th Son's 5th Son's 6th Son's 7th Son's 8th Son's

three to five pendants, called a "label," painted across his father's arms. When this son succeeded to the title upon his father's death the label was removed and he had the right to bear his father's arms "undifferenced."

Toward the end of the fifteenth century a set of charges was designed which an armiger's sons had to add to his arms, instead of changing the entire coat of arms. The eldest son still bore a label as before. The second son showed a crescent, the third a molet (star), the fourth a martlet, the fifth a ring, the sixth a fleur-de-lis, the seventh a rose, the eighth a cross moline, and the ninth an eight-petaled flower. What the tenth and later sons would bear on their shields was never stated; the heralds must have felt that they had amply taken care of the future.

As we have seen, the eldest son removed the label from his arms when his father died, but all the other sons kept their symbols or "cadences" for life, unless the eldest son died without a son; then the second son inherited his father's arms.

Though an armiger's daughter could display her father's arms on a lozenge, or diamond shape, or sometimes on a circle or an oval, she would never use a shield.

When a man who bore arms married a woman with a right to bear her father's arms, it was customary to display both by dividing the shield party per pale, placing the husband's arms in the dexter half and the wife's in the sinister half. Their children would not inherit their mother's arms, but would display only their father's, with the proper cadences.

However if the father of a married woman died without sons, she became his heiress. Her arms were displayed on a small escutcheon or shield, called the "escutcheon of pretence," in the center of her husband's shield of arms, instead of in party per pale. This was to show that he had inherited his father-in-law's arms and they would pass on to his children as well as his own arms.

In such a case they would not be displayed by im-

HOW FAMILY ARMS DESCENDED

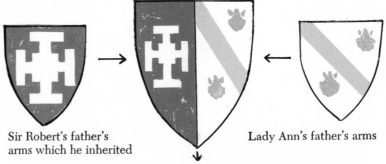

Sir Robert's father's
arms which he inherited

Lady Ann's father's arms

When he married Lady Ann, a non-heiress, Sir Robert's
arms were impaled with hers.

Sir Robert's eldest son's arms
with label. He did not inherit
his mother's arms.

palement, but by "quartering," dividing the shield into four segments by intersecting vertical and horizontal lines, with the father's arms in the first and fourth quarters, and the mother's in the second and third. If, however, the mother's family was more important than the father's, the order would be reversed, with her arms in the first and fourth quarters, and his in the second and third.

As families grew older, succeeding generations inherited more and more arms as they intermarried. Soon

Arms of his son Richard quartering his parents' arms

Sir Robert's arms, had he married Lady Margaret, an heiress

Arms of Lady Margaret's father who left no sons, so that she became his heiress.

Quartered arms of Sir Richard's son, Henry

Sir Richard's arms after marriage to Lady Mary

Arms of Lady Mary, also an heiress

there was no longer room on a quartered shield to display all of them, and so the quarters themselves were quartered until some shields began to look like crazy quilts. Displaying two or more coats of arms on a shield was called "marshalling." By this time, since shields were no longer important as identification on the field of battle, the complicated designs didn't matter, and they were often richly beautiful.

9.　BLAZONRY

Blazonry is the art of describing a coat of arms, by words alone, so accurately that an artist familiar with heraldry could draw an exact picture of it, with every object in it correctly drawn and placed, each in its proper colors.

The words used in blazonry will probably seem very odd to our modern ears, both in the names of the objects themselves and the order of the descriptions, but to anyone who understands heraldry they are very exact. If you learn and follow the basic rules of blazonry described in this book, you yourself can blazon the coats of arms illustrated here. Try covering up the descriptions printed under some of the coats of arms and see how many of them you can blazon correctly.

Following is the order in which a coat of arms is blazoned:

1. THE FIELD

This is the entire surface of the shield. Its tincture or metal is the first thing described in a blazon, and the word "field" is not mentioned, since that is understood. For example, "Azure a bend Or" means a blue field crossed by a gold diagonal stripe from upper left to lower right as you face the shield. "Per pale argent and gules" means a field divided vertically into two halves, the dexter half silver and the sinister half red.

2. PRINCIPAL CHARGE

After the field is described, the main charge laid on it is next mentioned. For example, "Or a saltire azure between four martlets sable" tells you that the field is

| The Field | Principal Charge | Lesser Charges | Lesser Devices on Principal Charge |

gold and that upon it is a cross shaped like an X, colored blue, with a black swallow in each of the four spaces around the cross. The saltire, being the principal charge, is described before the martlets.

3. LESSER CHARGES

The martlets mentioned above are the lesser charges and are described after the principal charge.

4. LESSER DEVICES ON PRINCIPAL CHARGE

Example: "Argent on a fess sable between two mullets (or molets) gules a lozenge Or." This means: On a silver shield a black horizontal stripe crosses the middle between two red stars with a golden diamond in the center of the black stripe. The "lozenge Or" is a lesser device placed on the principal charge and is thus described next.

5. BORDURES

Next described are the bordures (borders). Exam-

Bordures   Chief   Canton

**The Royal Arms of England during the Reign
of Queen Elizabeth II. 1952-**

Since 1837 quarterly I and IV for England, gules, three lions
passant gardant in pale Or, armed and langued azure. Second
quarter, Or a lion rampant within a double tressure fleury-
counter-fleury gules, for Scotland. Third quarter, azure, a
harp Or stringed argent for Northern Ireland.

**The Royal Arms of England during the Reign
of Richard II. 1377-1399**

Quarterly the ancient arms of France and England. The arms
of France in the first and fourth quarter azure semy of gold
fleurs-de-lis. The arms of England in the second and third
quarters gules three lions passant gardant Or.

ple: "Argent three church bells and a bordure azure," which means a silver shield on which are three blue church bells, the field surrounded by a border also of blue.

6. CHIEFS AND CANTONS

These are described after the bordures because they are always superimposed on them. Example of "chief": "Argent three calves statant sable, on a chief of the last a rose of the first." This translates to: A silver shield on which are placed three black standing calves, with a black horizontal stripe covering the top third of the shield, on which is placed a white rose.

Example of "canton": "Argent a cross gules in the first canton a sword erect of the last." This blazons as a shield with a silver field on which is placed a red cross. In a small canton or oblong forming the upper left-hand area of the field is placed a red sword pointing upward.

10. ARMS OF ROYALTY
AND OF FAMOUS MEN

The modern royal arms of England do not represent the families of the rulers themselves, but
rather the realms over which the sovereign rules or
ruled. The present royal arms bear the three lions of
England in the first and fourth quarter, the arms of
Scotland in the second, and the harp of northern Ireland in the third.

In earlier times the royal arms on the shield often
remained unchanged, sometimes for several hundred
years, even though the crown changed from one family
to another. The arms changed only when there was a
change in the realm over which the sovereign ruled.
It was only by changes in the crest, the supporters or
the badges that heraldry would tell who was ruling
during the period.

69

The Arms of Field Marshal Montgomery

Azure, two lions passant gardant between as many fleurs-de-lis in chief and one in base, and two trefoils in fess, all Or.

The Arms of Viscount Astor

Or, a falcon resting on a dexter hand couped at the wrist, proper, and gauntleted gules; in chief, two fleurs-de-lis of the last.

As we have seen, the first known arms on record were those given by Henry I to his son-in-law Geoffrey, Count of Anjou, consisting of two golden lions on a blue shield. After that, Henry II and Richard I used lions in their arms, so that the lion became the sign of royalty in England.

In 1340, Edward III, whose mother was Isabella, the daughter of Philip IV of France, began to use the arms of France along with the lions of England in his shield. The arms remained the same when Richard II (1377–1399) ascended the throne. The shield was quartered, with the ancient arms of France, azure semy of gold fleurs-de-lis, in the first and fourth quarters, and the second and third quarters gules with three golden lions passant gardant.

On the preceding pages there are shown two modern shields of arms granted to well-known men. The first shield shows the arms of a man who distinguished himself as one of the most skillful generals of World War II, who took command of the British Eighth Army in North Africa when it was being driven back toward Egypt by General Rommel's German Afrika Corps. Had General Rommel succeeded in reaching Cairo and the Suez Canal, he could have cut the lifeline of Allied transport to the east. Soon after, General Bernard Montgomery took command of the

SOLÆ NM VIRTUS 60 INVICTÆ

British army there, Rommel's forces were driven back and finally surrendered to the combined forces of Montgomery and the American army.

For his brilliant service to England he was made a field marshal and given a title and a coat of arms, as shown.

Viscount Astor, a descendant of an American family which pioneered in the fur trade in the American West, became a Briton, and for services to his adopted country was also granted a shield of arms.

Next we find an extremely elaborate coat of arms belonging to Sir Bernard Marmaduke Fitzalan Howard, Duke of Norfolk, and premier duke of England. His arms required four quarterings, representing the four important families from which he was descended: the Howards, the Brothertons, the Warrens and the Fitzalans.

Besides his dukedom, his earldom and his four baronies in England, he also inherited a barony in the Scottish peerage, was a Knight of St. John, the famous Knights Hospitalers, and Lord Lieutenant of Sussex. The Duke of Norfolk is the traditional Earl Marshal of England, and so directs the College of Heralds. The two gold batons in saltire, behind his shield, are his insignia as Earl Marshal.

Next we come upon two pages of military and naval

Arms of Admiral Sir John Hawkins
Granted in 1565

Sable, on a base wavy argent and azure, a lion passant Or, and in chief, three golden roundels, denoting the English lion crossing the seas and bringing back treasure of gold. In 1568, after capturing a Spanish treasure ship, he was granted a canton of augmentation Or, a scallop between two palmer's staves sable. This canton concealed one of the roundels.

Arms of Admiral Sir Francis Drake
Granted in 1581

Sable, a fess wavy argent between two silver estoiles, representing his course on the waters and the stars by which he
steered. The crest is a globe surmounted by a ship under sail
proper with gold hawsers by which the ship is drawn by a
hand from out of the clouds. On the ship a dragon gules,
with outspread wings, faces the hand.

heroes of bygone days. First are the arms of Admiral Sir John Hawkins, one of the great sea raiders of the sixteenth century, who attacked and captured the Spanish treasure galleons sailing from Spanish American ports in the New World to Cádiz or Seville. He also took part in the famous defense of England's shores against the mighty Spanish Armada.

Below Admiral Hawkins' arms are those of an even more famous admiral of British fleets during the sixteenth century. Sir Francis Drake was a naval commander whose name struck terror to the captains of the Spanish treasure galleons. He turned up in the Spanish Main, off the South American coast, even in the Pacific, to harry the Dons and capture their cargoes of gold bars, jewels, pieces of eight, and silver plate. According to legend, when the mighty Spanish Armada was sighted, bearing up the Channel with hundreds of sail gleaming against the misty horizon, Drake was playing bowls at Plymouth. Unruffled, he continued his game, remarking that there would be plenty of time to finish before he sailed out to beat the Dons.

On the next page are the three shields showing the augmentation of the arms of England's greatest naval hero, Sir Horatio Nelson, the man who defeated the great fleet of Napoleon in Egypt at the battle of the

Sir Horatio Nelson   Viscount Nelson   Earl Nelson

The Duke of Wellington

Earl Kitchener

Nile, which resulted in the marooning of the French army with no way to get back to France.

Below, left, are the arms of the Duke of Wellington, the British general who led the allied army which defeated the Grand Army of Napoleon at Waterloo, and so saved Europe from complete subjection to the French emperor.

Next to the duke's arms are those of a more modern British army general, famous for his recapture of Khartoum, taken by the Mahdi, in Africa. He was also commander in chief of the British army at the beginning of World War I, but died at sea when a warship on which he was traveling to Russia was torpedoed. This general was Horatio Herbert, Earl Kitchener.

Eton College   Oxford University   Harrow School

See of Canterbury   City of Liverpool

Worshipful Company of Distillers

Royal Mail Steamship Company

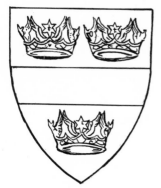

British European Airways

Badge of British Railways

Prudential Assurance Company

11. "DO-IT-YOURSELF" HERALDRY

You have now learned something of the history
and development of heraldry. You have seen how
an armiger tried to include in his arms symbols which
would reveal to everybody who understood heraldry

COAT OF ARMS FOR A SCHOOL CLASS

Argent a book expanded gules, over all a key palewise sable between numerals 6 and 5 in chief of the last.
Crest: a lamp of knowledge gules. Supporters two owls at gaze.

COAT OF ARMS FOR A BOYS' ROCKETRY CLUB

Azure a rocket Or palewise, discharging smoke argent and three flame jets gules in base, between two stars in chief of the third, all within a border of the second.
Crest: a moon in the first quarter Or.

COAT OF ARMS FOR A SAILING CLUB

Azure an anchor in pale, argent. In chief gules a rope knot
proper.
Crest: a lymphad sable, sail furled, flag and pennants flotant
to the sinister, the oars in action proper.

what his family stood for, who his forebears were, what deeds of courage they and he had accomplished. By his choice of the kind of beast, bird or plant or other symbols with which he charged his shield, one might read whether he was a mighty warrior, a man of the church or a quiet student.

You have seen that in England, churches, universities, schools, business houses, private clubs and associations and many others have been granted coats of arms which they proudly display whenever and wherever possible.

Wouldn't it be interesting to design a decorative coat of arms for your class, club, athletic team or just for yourself? Following the rules of heraldic custom as described in this book, such a coat of arms would perform the purposes of a real heraldic coat by showing in its bearings the activities and reasons for being of your class or club. Of course such arms would not pretend to be authentic arms registered by the College of Heralds, but they would certainly be handsomer and more original on a wall, a windbreaker, a sweat shirt or a jacket than a crude picture of an Indian head or crossed baseball bats.

A painted plywood shield would make an attractive decoration for a clubroom, or in each member's bedroom. The arms might appear on writing paper and

COATS OF ARMS FOR A BOY AND GIRL 4-H CLUB MEMBER

Boy's Arms: Gules mounted upon the trunk of a tree fess-wise eradicated and sprouting to the dexter proper, a bull passant argent pied and unguled sable, gorged with a collar and chain reflexed over the back and charged on the body with two fleur-de-lis.
Crest: a sheaf of wheat proper.

Girl's Arms: Vert a fleece proper fesswise between two apples Or in chief and in base, slipped and leaved, within a border of the last.

envelopes, or on a banner to hang on the wall or to fly from a staff above the clubhouse.

The arms might be a simple shield in one color, or a crest, inexpensive to print on stationery, or a more ambitious effort, with shield, helm, crest and supporters, and even an appropriate motto. The important thing would be to follow the rules of heraldry and to choose symbols which would express the aims and purposes of your group, or yourself.

In this chapter are several suggested coats of arms for a school class, an athletic club, a model rocket club, as well as several private coats of arms. These are only meant as a jumping-off point for your own ideas.

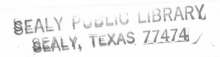

GLOSSARY

ARMIGER — One entitled to armorial bearings.

BEARINGS — Any one of the emblems or charges in an escutcheon or coat of arms.

BEND — A diagonal stripe from dexter chief to sinister base.

BEND SINISTER — *see* Bend; a diagonal stripe in the opposite direction.

BLAZONRY — The science of describing armorial bearings by words alone.

BORDURE — A border surrounding the shield.

CANTING ARMS — A coat of arms in picture form which illustrates a noble's name.

CHAIN MAIL — Flexible defensive armor of interlinked metal rings.

CHARGES — Emblems placed on the field of a shield of arms.

COAT OF ARMS — The armorial bearings of any person painted or embroidered on the surcoat.

COGNIZANCES — Heraldic bearings.

DEXTER — The right side of a shield of arms (bearer's right).

DIFFERENCING — Each son makes some change in his father's armorial bearings.

EMBLAZON — To inscribe or adorn with heraldic bearings.

ESCUTCHEON — The surface, usually shield-shaped, on which armorial bearings are displayed.

FESS — A horizontal stripe across a shield of arms.

FIELD — The surface of a shield.

HAUBERK — A coat of mail developed into a long tunic of chain mail.

HONORABLE ORDINARIES — Simple geometrically designed bearings.

JOUST — Combat on horseback between two knights with lances; as part of a tournament.

LABEL — A narrow bar with three to five pendants which the eldest son painted across his father's arms to achieve his own bearings, which was removed upon his father's death.

MARSHALLING — Displaying several coats of arms on one shield.

MEN-AT-ARMS — Knights who were hired out to a noble as a member of his private army.

PALE — A vertical stripe across a field of arms.

PIKEMEN — Foot soldiers.

PURSUIVANTS — Functionaries ranking below a herald, but having similar duties: junior heralds.

91

QUARTERING — Dividing the shield into four segments by intersecting vertical and horizontal lines.

SALTIRE — A charge consisting of a cross shaped like an X.

SEMÉ or SEMY — A variation in arms achieved by scattering the field with small objects in a pattern.

SHIELD OF ARMS — The face of a shield on which arms are displayed.

SINISTER — Left side of the shield (bearer's left).

STANDARD — A long narrow tapering flag used by a noble or leader on special occasions.

SUPPORTERS — A figure of a man or animal, placed one on each side of the shield.

SURCOAT — A tuniclike coat worn over armor.

TABARD — A loose coat worn by a herald blazoned with his lord's arms on the front, back and sleeves.

TINCTURES — Colors used in armorial bearings.

TORSE — A wreath of twisted silk resting on top of the helm.

VASSAL — Subject, one who has placed himself under the protection of another as his lord.

INDEX

93

Kings of Heralds, *see* Kings of Arms
knight, attire of, 14, 26, 29; in battle, 18; shields of, 14, 31, 47
Knight of St. John, 74
Knights Hospitalers, 74
Knights of the Garter, 23

label, 59
Lancaster, 25
lesser charges, 65
lion, positions on shield, 40, 54
lozenge, 33, 59

mantlet, 50
mantling, 29
marshalling, 62
martlet, 50, 65
molet, 59
moline, 59
"monsters," 50
Montgomery, General Bernard, 72, 74

Nelson, Sir Horatio, 77
Norfolk, Duke of, 25, 74
Norroy and Ulster King of Arms, 25

pale, 44
party fields, 44
Philip IV, king of France, 72
pile, 45
Portcullis, 25
principal charge, 64-65
"pursuivants," *see* junior heralds

quartering, 27, 61-62, 72

Richard I, king of England, 72
Richard II, king of England, 72
Richard III, king of England, 23
Richmond, 25
ring, 59
Rouge Croix, 25
Rouge Dragon, 25

saltire, 45, 65
semé, 45
shield of arms, 25, 26, 39-40
shields, 15, 18, 19, 22, 25, 26, 29, 30-33, 34, 47, 50, 56, 57, 59, 60, 61-62, 72, 87, 89
"sinister" side, 39, 60
Somerset, 25
staffs, 15
stag, positions on shield, 55
standards, 15
supporters, 30, 69

tabard, 19
tinctures, 27, 34, 37, 64
torse, 30
tournaments, 18, 19, 22, 25, 26
trees, in heraldic design, 56
trumpeters, 22

war-horses, 25
Wellington, Duke of, 79
William, Duke, 11, 14
William the Conqueror, 15
Windsor, 25

York, 25

94

Other Books by Walter Buehr

Through the Locks: Canals Today and Yesterday
Treasure: The Story of Money and Its Safeguarding
Harbors and Cargoes
Ships of the Great Lakes
Trucks and Trucking
Knights, Castles and Feudal Life
Railroads Today and Yesterday
Cargoes in the Sky
The Crusaders
Sending the Word: The Story of Communications
The Genie and the Word: Electricity and Communication
Keeping Time
The Story of the Wheel
The World of Marco Polo
The French Explorers in America
The Spanish Armada
The Spanish Conquistadores in North America
Chivalry and the Mailed Knight
Westward — With American Explorers

The Author

WALTER BUEHR is an author-illustrator whose books on knighthood and other historical subjects remain favorites with young people. His three previous books on the feudal era include *The Crusaders, Knights and Castles and Feudal Life,* and *Chivalry and the Mailed Knight.* His books on the exploration of the Americas include *The French Explorers in America, The Spanish Conquistadores in North America,* and *Westward With American Explorers.* He has also written and illustrated numerous books dealing with commerce and industry. Mr. Buehr and his wife Camilla, a portrait painter, divide their time between Abaco in the Bahamas, and Noroton, Connecticut.

This book may be kept
FOURTEEN DAYS
A fine will be charged for each
day the book is kept overtime.

FEB 4			
FEB 2 8 198			
AUG 5 1981			
JAN 1 8 1982			
JUL 5 1983			

Demco 38-293